Echoes of Joy: A Devotional for Animal Lovers

Staci Mauney

Echoes of Joy: A Devotional for Animal Lovers
©2018 Staci Mauney

Cover Design: Linda Boulanger
www.telltalebookcovers.com
Interior Format & Design: Staci Mauney
http://prestigeprose.com

ISBN: 9781719976916

Introduction

I grew up with pets, from a parakeet to cats to dogs. Rescuing animals was a regular part of my childhood. When I was thirteen and my brother was nine, we rescued a litter of bunnies after their mother was killed. We fed them with a bottle and made a little bed out of a shoebox for them.

Caring for other creatures came naturally to us. It started with parents who shared their love of living creatures with us. We learned at an early age not to assume that other people would help. It was our responsibility to take care of these animals, whether that meant giving them a home or feeding them until they were strong enough to go back into the wild. By raising a variety of pets, I learned many lessons that I wouldn't have learned on my own.

Similarities abound between our relationship with Jesus and between us and our pets. As animal lovers, we can grow as Christians and strengthen our relationship with Jesus by learning from our pets.

Owning a pet has many benefits, from reducing stress, anxiety, and loneliness to improving overall health. I have received these benefits myself, and I wrote this devotional to share those benefits and the lessons I've learned. I hope these messages encourage you in your walk with Christ and bring you joy as you consider the wonders of the animals with which we have been entrusted.

Author's Note: All Scripture quotations are taken from the New International Version (NIV) unless otherwise noted.

Day 1
Calming an Anxious Heart

"Do not be anxious about anything, but in every situation, by prayer and petition, with thanksgiving, present your requests to God." (Phil 4:6)

Lilly, my Yorkshire terrier, has separation anxiety. It's plagued her since she was a puppy. When I would leave for work, I could hear her nails click-clacking across the floor as she ran to hide under my bed. Over time, she adjusted to our routine.

Now that I work from home, I see signs of her separation anxiety coming back. If I leave for a significant amount of time during the day, I know I'll have a shadow when I get home.

To relieve some of her anxiety, I leave the TV and lights on when I'm gone. I take her for walks and for rides in the car when I go through a drive through. She rides in the backseat, happy as can be, barking at random passersby.

Like Lilly, we can let anxiety get the best of us when we feel uncertain or face a new situation. I'm not qualified to speak about anxiety as a medical condition. But I can speak about anxiety as an emotion that threatens to overwhelm us. I've faced that type of anxiety, and it can stop us from making decisions, interacting with others, or moving forward. It can be very isolating.

When we face situations that cause us to worry or fret, we should give thanks instead. Offering thanks for a difficult situation seems contrary to our natural reaction, which is to turn inward and focus on the problem. When we give thanks for the blessings in our lives—even those stressful situations—our eyes turn from our worries and onto God and the good things he has done for us.

The Lord gives us peace and calms our anxiety when we let him: "Let the peace of Christ rule in your hearts, since as members of one body you were called to peace. And be thankful" (Col 3:15). We should cling to him as he takes our fears away. And we will feel his peace, no matter our circumstances.

Dear Jesus, thank you for calming my anxious thoughts. You provide peace that passes all understanding when I give you my worries. Help me to always give thanks and turn my attention from myself and onto you. Amen.

Day 2
Fear Is a Thief

"For I am the Lord your God who takes hold of your right hand and says to you, Do not fear; I will help you." (Is 41:13)

In high school, rodeo events fascinated me. The challenges seemed daring and fun. My uncle participated in calf roping, and one of my friends was a barrel racer. My friend and her family invited me to tag along to several of her events. I loved watching the competitors ride their horses around the yard as they got ready to compete. I stayed on the sidelines, enjoying the atmosphere and hanging out with my friend.

After much cajoling, my friend convinced me to ride her horse. I was hesitant because I'd been on the back of a horse only a couple of times. But I climbed on, and she gave me a quick riding lesson.

I took off and promptly turned the horse toward a tree. I heard my friend yelling at me to pull up on the reins. When I did, the horse walked backward. I didn't even know it could do that! I pointed it toward an open, grassy area between a couple of trailers. I took off again, tapping my heels to the horse's flank. It quickly increased its pace to a canter, and I leaned back from the unexpected force. I pulled up on the reins slightly, and the horse slowed, finally stopping in front of my friend.

My friend protested as I dismounted, asking me to try again. I refused. Even though no one paid attention to me, I felt self-conscious about my lack of ability in a crowd of experienced horsemen and women. I felt afraid that people would see me as an imposter, and I let my fear of failure get in the way of learning something new that day—something that could have potentially been lots of fun had I stuck with it.

Fear is a thief that robs us of our joy. Instead of focusing on the positive that day, I chose to focus on the negative, and I allowed fear to take the lead. While I still struggle with fear, I have learned to turn my focus to Jesus when fear starts to take over. Even today, my initial reaction when faced with an unfamiliar situation is to retreat. But I've learned to pause before saying no. Using this practice has led me to learn new things over the years, and it was crucial in meeting new people and creating a community for myself when I moved from a small town to a large city.

With the Lord's help, I can let go of my fear and let him lead me where he wants me to go. He will show me the way when I turn things over to him.

Dear Jesus, thank you for showing me how to let go of my fear. When fear strikes again, and it will, help me to remember that you are always with me, and your faithfulness will see me through every situation I face. Amen.

Day 3
Learning Responsibility

... "for each one should carry their own load." (Gal 6:5)

When I was eight years old, I chose a cocker spaniel puppy from the litter at my aunt's house. I named her Tanny, and she was our new pet. She was a constant companion during my childhood years. I trimmed her hair when it flopped into her eyes and otherwise tortured her with my inept attempts at grooming. Baths were the worst. She hated them with a passion, and I learned to keep my distance when my dad gave her a bath so that I wouldn't get drenched.

Having a dog at a young age helped me learn responsibility. Even though the primary responsibility for Tanny fell to my dad, I helped him make sure she had food and water, that she played and ran around during the day, and that she was home safe in her pen at night.

Learning to care for something other than myself has been a lesson I've taken with me throughout my life. Taking care of Tanny taught me the importance of planning her meals and exercise routine. I also learned to plan far enough ahead to ask someone to take care of her if we left for an extended time. Having a dog made it easier for me to interact with people—I had no shortage of stories about Tanny's antics, and almost everyone I knew could relate to stories about a funny, stubborn dog.

Tanny also got me out of the house. I preferred to stay inside to read, but she stayed outside. My brother and I spent countless hours playing with her. We walked or rode bikes to my grandparents' house almost every day except for the coldest days in the winter. Every time we made the half-mile trip across town, Tanny ran along beside us.

Looking back, I can see the fundamental role that having a dog played in creating the person I am today. My parents didn't let me shirk my duty of caring for her, and through her, I learned the value of animals and the benefits of hard work. She was a good dog, and I still miss her crooked grin and floppy ears.

Dear Jesus, thank you for pets and the value they bring to our lives. Help me to remember the lessons of responsibility and dependability I learned by caring for them. Thank you for the time that I had with the special pets in my life. Amen.

Day 4
Curious Lilly

"There the angel of the Lord appeared to him in flames of fire from within a bush. Moses saw that though the bush was on fire it did not burn up. So Moses thought, 'I will go over and see this strange sight—why the bush does not burn up.'" (Ex 3:2-3)

As I put my groceries away, I heard rustling behind me. I turned to see Lilly with her head in the plastic grocery sack, sniffing the items still inside. She backed away as I called her name.

Whether it's sticking her head in a sack or my purse or charging from a blade of grass to a rock to another blade of grass, Lilly is a very curious dog. She loves to explore and find new things, and she doesn't like closed doors. If I leave a door open just a crack, I see Lilly's nose sticking through, followed by the rest of her little body as she bumps the door open. Often, when I close the door to my office to work, I hear light scratching on the other side and a snuffling sigh as she realizes she can't get inside.

I believe that God made us all with a natural curiosity that, when channeled correctly, will lead to great things: new inventions and discoveries and learning more about his wonderful creation. My own natural curiosity has led me to a career in which I'm constantly learning new things. When we don't channel our curiosity correctly, we can get ourselves into trouble. We find ourselves pursuing our own paths that are contrary to God's leading.

Like Moses in Exodus 3, we can use our natural curiosity to examine Scripture and the nature of God. While there are things that we will never know (Ps 145:3), we can know more about the nature of God. When we ask, he will show us how to use our natural curiosity to draw closer to him. He will reveal verses in Scripture that bear out his nature. He will also reveal himself in other ways: through nature, music, books, movies, and the words of others. If we are open to hearing from him, we will hear his voice no matter the method.

Dear Lord, thank you for giving us the gift of curiosity, which allows us to discover new things and learn more about you. Amen.

Day 5
What's in a Name?

"'The virgin will conceive and give birth to a son, and they will call him Immanuel' (which means 'God with us').'" (Mt 1:23)

Lilly came to live with me when she was six months old, and she already had her name. I kept it because she answered to it, and I liked it. When I was just eight years old, I named my childhood dog Tanny because of her color. At age five, I had a parakeet named Sue Ellen in a cage in my bedroom. Apparently, I picked up the name when my mom and my grandma watched *Dallas*.

People have always struggled with my name. I've been called Tracy so many times I've lost count. I've also been called Samantha and Stephanie. Maybe it's the "s" at the beginning of my name, or maybe I don't look like a "Staci" to that person. I've answered to all these names, but having experienced this makes it especially important for me to get others' names right. I'm never more embarrassed than when I call someone by the wrong name.

Names are important. They identify who we are, and we identify with what we're called. If we're called loser, broken, or defeated, then we identify with those names.

What does God call us? Among other good things, he calls us his masterpiece (Eph 2:10 NLT), beautiful (Song 4:7), his child (Jn 1:12), his friend (Jn 15:15), an heir with Christ (Rom 8:17), and made in his image (Gen 1:27; Eph 4:24). When we believe we are what he says we are, our lives will be changed. Our perspective and how we view others and the world around us changes, and we will start to see others as God sees them.

Dear Jesus, thank you for calling me yours. Help me to believe that I am who you say I am and that I belong to you. In you, I'm made whole. Amen.

Day 6
The Power Within Us

"From the ends of the earth I call to you, I call as my heart grows faint; lead me to the rock that is higher than I." (Ps 61:2)

Lilly barked incessantly from the backyard. I had gone back inside the house to do dishes, and I could see her from the kitchen window as she stood and barked. However, I couldn't see what had her attention. I went back outside, and as I approached her, I saw a turtle that had withdrawn into its shell. She barked furiously, sure that this strange creature represented a threat.

When we become overwhelmed by our circumstances, we become like Lilly: defensive and trying to protect what we think is ours. But everything we have belongs to God: our time, our money, our families (Ps 24:1; 1 Chron 29:14). Perhaps we've overcommitted, and our schedule threatens to overwhelm us. Perhaps we need to have a conversation with someone about a difficult subject, and we are unsure of the outcome. Perhaps we're facing a health crisis or grief at the loss of a loved one.

When we turn our eyes back to God, he will help us carry our burdens. The threat may still be there, but when we look at it through God's eyes, we can see it for what it is. It only has power over us if we give it power. We should focus on the power of Christ within us—this same power that allowed him to rise from the grave, and this same power that allows us to rise above our fears. When we give our fears to God and draw on the power he gives us, he will sustain us.

Dear Jesus, thank you for overcoming death on a cross so that I can be an overcomer as well. Thank you for putting our fears into perspective. Help us to draw on your power when facing the threats in our lives. Amen.

Day 7

A Change in Perspective

"There is neither Jew nor Gentile, neither slave nor free, nor is there male and female, for you are all one in Christ Jesus." (Gal 3:28)

For a while, I lived down the street from my uncle and aunt. My uncle had a horse barn on the property behind me. If the horses were out when I took Lilly outside, she would tug on her leash until she reached them, wagging her tail the entire way. Once she reached the fence, the horses would bend down so that she could touch noses with them.

Lilly knew that the horses were different from her, but she didn't care. She recognized a fellow animal and connected on a fundamental level. They were both gentle and accepting of the other.

The Bible speaks on diversity and has strong words for how we should treat others, whether rich or poor, male or female, Christian or non-Christian (Js 2:5-7, Gal 3:28, Rm 2:11).

When we look at others, we tend to notice our differences first: hair color, eye color, skin color, gender. If we take time to get to the know the person better, we will discover other differences, perhaps in culture, the church (or lack of) we were raised in, type of education, and abilities and hobbies.

As Christians, we face issues that divide us. But if we can have a conversation instead of a confrontation over these issues, we might learn to understand why we believe the things we do and to refrain from judgment. When we ask the Lord for help, we can see from the other person's point of view and understand that person better by having compassion for what he or she has been through.

Dear Jesus, thank you that you have created all of us equal in your sight through the shedding of your blood. You do not see our differences; you see only that we are your children. You love us all the same and shower your mercy and grace on us in equal measures. Help us to do the same with those around us. Amen.

Day 8
The Lost One

"Or suppose a woman has ten silver coins and loses one. Doesn't she light a lamp, sweep the house and search carefully until she finds it? And when she finds it, she calls her friends and neighbors together and says, 'Rejoice with me; I have found my lost coin.'" (Lk 15:8-9)

I walked around the yard with the flashlight, calling Lilly's name and feeling panic rise in my chest. She had escaped. Again. Her leash was gone, meaning she had somehow worked it loose so that she could run away. Or someone had taken her. I couldn't let myself think of what that might mean.

I listened closely, but didn't hear anything. No barking. No whining. I took off down the street, still calling her name. One of my friends came to help and called for her, but still nothing. As I walked back into the yard, my mom came running over. When I told her I hadn't found Lilly, my mom grabbed my hands and began to pray that God would lead us to my little dog.

A few moments later, my dad walked up with Lilly in his arms. Relieved, I said a prayer of thanks and hugged Lilly, shedding a few tears of joy that she'd been found. She wiggled around and licked my face, happy to see me.

My dad had found her in the neighbor's driveway. Her leash had caught under the tire of the neighbor's vehicle when she ran beneath it. She didn't get far. But because she wouldn't bark, we couldn't find her.

This reminds me of the story Jesus told in which a man who lost one sheep left the other ninety-nine to search for the one that was lost (Lk 15:4-7). In another example given by

Jesus, a woman lost a penny and turned the entire house upside down to find it (Lk 15:8).

That's how I felt about Lilly. And that's how God feels about us. He will look for us and pursue us until he finds us. But he won't force us to come to him.

We may feel we're caught by the cares of this world—health issues or choices we've made—and we're afraid to run to him. He will always take us back and love us no matter what we've done. When we realize that and truly understand it in our hearts, we will find our way back to him.

Dear Jesus, thank you for leaving the ninety-nine to look for us—the one who was lost. Thank you that you love us all uniquely and individually. Help us to turn to you. Amen.

Day 9
The Good Steward

"The Lord sustains them on their sickbed and restores them from their bed of illness." (Ps 41:3)

I stretched from the plank pose into the down dog position in yoga. Lilly danced around me, trying to lick my face. As I stretched, she ran under my arms to get a better angle. I laughed and stood up. She backed away, watching to see what I would do next. I moved back into the pose, and then she imitated me and stretched into down dog as well. Laughing again, I stood and petted her on the head.

I believe that God desires for us to take care of ourselves. I like to walk and do yoga stretches. But there are times that I've fallen away from this and don't do much at all. I eat well for a time, and then I overindulge in sweets.

Recently, a round of routine checkups at the doctor's office yielded abnormal results. These results took me by surprise as I realized I had prided myself on being a good steward of my health—and yet here I was with a compromised immune system. Running my business by myself was, at times, exhausting. Each day, I ran full speed ahead, tackling the projects and problems that day brought.

The phone call from the doctor delivering unexpected test results made me pause and consider what my schedule was doing to my body. Yes, I needed to work. Yes, I felt called to work—to write and spread the love of Jesus through the written word. But I needed to take better care of myself so that I could continue to do this work. With Jesus' help, I would make the changes necessary to find time to rest and take care of myself so that I could continue to tell others about his great love for us.

Dear Jesus, help me to be a good steward of my health and to take care of my body. Thank you for drawing my attention to the damage I was doing before it was too late. Help me to rest so that I can fulfill my calling of showing others your love. Amen.

Day 10
Give Your Cares to God

*"Indeed, the very hairs of your head are all numbered.
Don't be afraid; you are worth more than many sparrows."
(Lk 12:7)*

I watched the birds flit through the air in my backyard.
A cardinal sat in the tree nearest the house. Its red feathers
stood out among the branches and leaves of the tree. Some
believe that cardinals represent the spirits of those who have
passed. Maybe one of my grandparents or my uncle had
come to visit. Others believe that a cardinal sighting for a
single person may signal a future romantic encounter. I like
that idea, too.

A blue jay rested in the yard, its blue feathers bright
against the green grass. Robins pecked the ground, looking
for grubs and worms that the recent rain had brought to the
surface. I walked back to my office, but even there, I heard
the chirp of the birds, so I opened the blind to watch as the
birds and squirrels chased each other around the yard.

One of my favorite verses in the Bible has always been
Matthew 6:26-27: "Look at the birds of the air; they do not
sow or reap or store away in barns, and yet your heavenly
Father feeds them. Are you not much more valuable than
they? Can any one of you by worrying add a single hour to
your life?"

The Father's love and care for us never ceases to amaze
me. I'm a worrier, and it's a characteristic of which I'm not
proud. Over the years, I've struggled to give my cares to
God. I hold too tightly to the things of this world that weigh
me down.

As I've gotten older, I've learned that it's the focus of my cares that matters. I can choose to focus on the problem, or I can choose to trust that God will provide a solution. Jesus isn't saying that we'll never have concerns, but with his help, we can focus on the eternal hope he provides. When I pray and read his word, my focus moves away from myself and my worries and onto God and his promises for my life.

As I watched the birds play in the backyard, I understood the meaning of this verse in a new way. I cling to the promise that God cares for me and will take care of me— all of me. I said a quick prayer of thanks for the beautiful reminder. Things won't always be easy, and I will have worries that press in on me. But the Lord will always be there, providing good things.

Dear Jesus, help me to trust you with the worries that press in every day. Help me to remember what your word says and to take everything to you, no matter how big or how small. Thank you for always providing everything I need when I need it. Amen.

Day 11
Comfort for the Hurting

"Who comforts us in all our troubles, so that we can comfort those in any trouble with the comfort we ourselves receive from God." (2 Cor 1:4)

Lilly has a weak stomach and often feels sick. She'll eat anything, which isn't a good combination. When she doesn't feel well, I try to comfort her and help her through her suffering by keeping her company and offering things I know she enjoys. I spread out several blankets on the furniture for her, and I sit with her in my recliner with a blanket over my legs even in the hottest part of the summer because I know that's her favorite place to be.

In the same way, when I don't feel well, I have friends and family who will check on me, bring me soup, and help me get back on my feet. For many years, I resisted asking for help, especially when I would get a migraine. Migraines are debilitating and made me feel weak, both physically and emotionally. I wanted to be left alone, and I wrongly believed that if I didn't ask for help, then I was fine, and the migraine wouldn't consume me. This faulty thought process caused me to suffer alone during these painful bouts for many years due to my own stubborn choices.

Now, I realize help is available and necessary to keep my spirits up. Chronic pain is debilitating, but having people around me who will help when I need them makes all the difference.

The Lord comforts us when we don't feel well or when it seems that nothing in our lives is going the way we want. He provides help through numerous avenues: a hug from a friend, a listening ear when I'm anxious, a song that lifts my spirits, or a line in a book or on a TV show that resonates with me.

We receive comfort from him so that we can, in turn, comfort others. Kind words or an encouraging text with Scripture can help soothe the ache that others feel when they are hurting. When I offer such things to others, I feel my own spirits lifting as well. Sometimes we resist being comforted by others, but by allowing others to enter our suffering with us, we will experience more fully the sense of community that God designed. When we turn to God for comfort, he will lift us up and help us through.

Dear Jesus, please comfort us so that we, in turn, can comfort others. Help us to recognize when we need to allow others to comfort us. And help us to recognize when others need us. Amen.

Day 12
The Houdini Dog

"I will establish your borders from the Red Sea to the Mediterranean Sea, and from the desert to the Euphrates River. I will give into your hands the people who live in the land, and you will drive them out before you." (Ex 23:31)

The first few days we had her, Tanny, my childhood pet, lived in a big pen my dad built in the backyard just for her. When we played outside, my brother and I would let her out into the yard to romp around with us and our friends.

Tanny loved the freedom of playing outside her pen. The first time she got out, I couldn't believe it. We couldn't find any holes in the ground, so we knew she hadn't dug her way out. My dad watched her for a few days and then caught her in the act: she had climbed up the corner of the fence. He placed a board over the corner of her pen so that she couldn't climb out anymore. But the next day, she escaped again. Like Spiderman, she scampered up the middle of the fence and jumped down into the yard right in front of us. Even though I was aggravated that she kept getting out, I admired her gumption and wanted a little of it for myself.

Just as my dad built Tanny's pen to keep her safe, God provides boundaries to keep us safe as well. Tanny's escapades presented an opportunity for her to be hurt as well as us if anything happened to her. We do not live in a vacuum, and our actions always affect others, even though we may not realize the full extent of the impact.

In Psalm 16:6, King David said, "The boundary lines have fallen for me in pleasant places; surely I have a delightful inheritance." While God gives us free will, he also gives us boundaries to protect us. Some boundaries protect us from ourselves while others protect us from those around us.

As followers of Christ, we know that we can trust God to have our best interests at heart. When he places a boundary around us, he does so for a reason. When we learn to trust him fully and surrender our control to him, we will see the rewards of remaining within those boundaries far outweigh pursuing our own path.

Dear Jesus, thank you for the blessing of staying within the boundaries you have set for us. The benefits far outweigh anything we could have imagined on our own. Help us to trust you with the boundaries you have placed in our lives. Amen.

Day 13
Lingering with Lilly

"Be joyful in hope, patient in affliction, faithful in prayer." (Rom 12:12)

Lilly pulled me down the street, tugging hard at her leash. She stopped abruptly to sniff around the bottom of the neighbor's trash can. She walked two steps and sniffed a spot on the ground, and then wandered into the road to sniff a piece of gravel. Satisfied, she took off again, only to careen into the yard two houses down to sniff something in the grass.

The rest of our walk continued in much the same way—a series of starts and stops as Lilly wandered as far as her leash would allow. As she lingered over another invisible scent on the ground, I grew impatient to move on. I had a purpose: to exercise. But Lilly had a different, perhaps better, purpose: to enjoy herself.

Walking with Lilly put my patience to the test. I wanted to get my steps in and finish the course so that I could get on with my day. But Lilly had no need of such things. The more I walked with Lilly, the more I understood the value of waiting and lingering over the small things.

Over the years, I have asked the Lord for many things for which he has asked me to wait. His answer hasn't been no, but I haven't heard "yes" yet, either. I wait for healing from migraines, for physical and emotional healing for family and friends, for direction about working with a particular client, for guidance about a big financial decision—and the list goes on.

According to Galatians 5:22-23 (NLT), patience is a fruit of the spirit: "But the Holy Spirit produces this kind of fruit in our lives: love, joy, peace, patience, kindness, goodness, faithfulness, gentleness, and self-control. There is no law against these things!" As believers, we all have these fruits within us, and we can ask God to help them grow.

Most people don't want to ask for patience, knowing that patience will then be required of them. But whether we ask or not, situations arise in which we must exercise patience. How we respond is up to us.

We can learn to take advantage of the wait. I have learned to walk in place while Lilly explores. Although I'm still waiting, I'm being active during the delay, and we can do the same as we wait on the Lord. We can read his word, pray, and gather with other believers. And as we wait, we will grow and become the person he wants us to be.

Dear Jesus, I pray that the fruit of patience will continue to grow in me as I wait for you to move. Thank you for providing situations in which your fruit can grow in me. Amen.

Day 14
A Few of Lilly's Favorite Things

"Whoever finds their life will lose it, and whoever loses their life for my sake will find it." (Mt 10:39)

Lilly's favorite thing in the whole world is a fuzzy blanket. I think she loves fuzzy blankets even more than she loves me. If I sit down and don't cover up with a blanket, she will find another place to sit—one covered by a blanket.

I have favorite things, too. Favorite books and favorite hobbies and favorite restaurants. I don't want to give up my favorite things, either. In fact, I have an entire room full of books—as well as several electronic readers. I own more books than I could ever read in a million lifetimes.

Sometimes, God asks us to give up our favorite things so that he can make room for new, better things. Thankfully, he hasn't asked me to give up my books, but he has asked me to give up hobbies such as cross stitching, which I dearly loved. The close eye work contributed to my migraines, so I finally gave it up.

He's also asked me to give up people who have taken his place in my life. I struggled to give up a friendship that had turned toxic. Even though I knew God wanted me to let go, I continued to hang onto the friendship, thinking things would improve.

Eventually, I did let go of the relationship, and God replaced that friendship with a wonderful community of strong women who love and support me for who I am. When God asks us to give something up, it is for our good, even if we can't see it at the time because "…we know that in all things God works for the good of those who love him, who have been called according to his purpose" (Rom 8:28).

Dear Jesus, help us to give up things—or people—we love, but who are causing us harm or drawing us away from you. Your word says you will work this out for our good, and I'm trusting you to bring me something better. Amen.

Day 15
The Destruction of Jealousy

"You are still worldly. For since there is jealousy and quarreling among you, are you not worldly? Are you not acting like mere humans?" (I Cor 3:3)

A calico cat we named Kitty adopted my parents. She follows my mom around the yard and plops down to have her belly rubbed like a dog. Watching Kitty follow Lilly around the yard is pretty comical. Lilly tolerates Kitty by turning her head and pretending the cat isn't there. Kitty will touch her nose to Lilly's or sneak up behind Lilly, causing my little dog to leap away and start barking. If I pet the cat, I get an earful from Lilly.

Lilly and Kitty remind me of jealous siblings who endure each other's presence. The Bible contains stories about several sibling rivalries: Cain and Abel (Gen 4), Jacob and Esau (Gen 27), and Joseph and his brothers (Gen 37). In each case, jealousy destroyed the relationship between siblings. Cain's jealousy toward Abel's sacrifice led him to murder his brother. Jacob, jealous of his father Isaac's preferential treatment of Esau, plotted with his mother to steal Esau's birthright. Joseph, who faced his brothers' jealousy because of his father's favoritism, was sold into slavery by his brothers.

A complex emotion, jealousy usually kicks in when we feel threatened. If allowed to grow unfettered, it will destroy even the strongest relationships. It creates issues of distrust and insecurity. It's a natural, human emotion, and we can't control it on our own. When faced with disappointment in our human relationships, we can turn to God, who will never leave us. With his help, we can let go of our jealousy to see others as he sees them and to show them his love.

Dear Jesus, help me to let go of any jealousy that I feel. I can't do that on my own. Show me how to love the way you love. Amen.

Day 16
A Way Through the Pain

"May your unfailing love be my comfort, according to your promise to your servant." (Ps 119:76)

I heard the screen door open and the mail slot squeak. As the mail carrier opened the door to shove the mail through the slot, Lilly barked and charged at the door, grabbing the mail as it came through the slot. She slung the mail across the room and ran head-first into the door as she tried to get to the offender who dared to invade our space.

I grabbed the mail and moved Lilly away from the door before she hurt herself. But I got there too late. She bumped into my leg on her way back to the door, and then she froze. I stooped to pet her so that I could see what had happened. She curled up and wanted me to rub her belly. Then she licked her lips. I examined her mouth and saw a loose tooth. She hung her head and licked her lips some more. I could tell she was in pain, so I picked her up and carried her around the house, trying to soothe her.

Lilly hadn't needed a vet since we'd moved from my hometown, so I called my vet back home. He told me I could try to pull the tooth myself. Yikes. I didn't want to hurt her further, so I called my best friend. She came over, took one look at Lilly's tooth, and called her vet for me. They got us in right away, and an hour later, Lilly was pain-free and ready to play again.

When I thought about how much pain Lilly was in, I hurt, too. How much more must God hurt when we, his children, hurt! He not only sees our pain, but feels what we feel. He cries with us. And he comforts us. Whether it's a perfectly timed song on the radio, a friend who's willing to drop everything to lend a listening ear, a pet who curls up next to you to keep you company, or a beautiful sunrise, God pursues us and provides comfort to us. And because we know what it's like to receive this comfort, we are able to pass that on to others when they need it.

Dear Jesus, thank for being there through my pain and sending others to comfort me. Amen.

Day 17
Focus on God, Not Fear

"When I am afraid, I put my trust in you." (Ps 56:3)

During the hottest part of the summer, I woke up at 6:00 a.m. to walk Lilly. Even though we left early, the temperature had already risen into the low 80s. Oklahoma summers can be brutal. One of the parks where we walk has a pretty fountain on one end. On this particular day, we walked to the fountain, climbed down the steps, and circled the fountain a couple of times. Lilly jumped up on the edge of the fountain, peered into the water, and promptly jumped in, startling me and herself. She resurfaced and paddled for the edge, but she was too small to get out on her own. I lifted her out of the water, and she took off running at full speed to dry off, dragging me behind her as I held onto her leash with all my strength.

In much the same way that Lilly leaped without fear into the pool at the bottom of the fountain, Jesus calls us to take leaps of faith every day. Some tasks require small, baby steps while others require giant leaps. For me, moving to the big city and changing careers—at the same time—required faith that I didn't have when I was not as mature in my spiritual walk.

We can easily allow fear to hold us back. Sometimes fear keeps us in the same place too long, while it can move us in the wrong direction at other times. For many years, I allowed fear to rule my life and make decisions for me. I put off pursuing my calling of writing. And I wouldn't even talk about moving to the big city—the thought of such a big change overwhelmed me.

But God pursued me and continued to whisper to my heart. Over time, I listened to him instead of the fear. Even so, I still have a tendency to let fear creep into my heart when I'm faced with adversity or a new situation. When that happens, I have difficulty making a decision. When I let fear control me, the enemy, Satan, has me right where he wants me—focused on my situation instead of on God. When I focus, I can hear God's still, small voice drowning out the clamoring cry of fear. No matter what I face, I know he will not leave me. He will continue to work in my heart until all I can hear is his voice.

Dear Jesus, thank you for pursuing me and speaking to me even when my focus is on my fear and the situation in which I find myself. Help me to hear your voice over all others. Amen.

Day 18
Waiting in the Wings

"But as for me, I will look to the Lord; I will wait for the God of my salvation; my God will hear me." (Mc 7:7)

Lilly stood on all fours on the back of the couch, growling low in her throat and looking toward the door. Her growl grew in intensity until it developed into a full-blown bark, almost drowning out the chime of the doorbell. She bounded off the couch and raced to the door, alternately scratching and jumping at the door, barking the entire time. I grabbed my bowl of candy off the table near the door, took a deep breath, and opened the door.

"Trick or treat!" the kids in superhero costumes yelled, holding out their sacks for candy.

Lilly jumped at the screen door, trying with all of her might to push through the door. The kids jumped back, and then I heard, "What a cute puppy!" So much for her ferociousness.

I asked the kids to go around to the front of the house. (I used the side door as my entry.) Lilly stayed right on my heels, determined to get to these kids who had the nerve to come to our house on Halloween. I made her stay inside while I stepped onto the enclosed porch. With a barrier now between Lilly and the kids, I handed out candy without fear of Lilly jumping on the kids or running away through the open door.

Isn't our walk with God often like this? Like Lilly, we see something that we want, and we try desperately to reach it. We may face obstacles that keep us from getting it. Maybe we're after something that isn't good for us. Or maybe we simply need to learn to wait.

One of the most difficult things God asks us to do is wait. While we wait, we experience impatience, we wrestle with God, and we feel at odds with what we need versus what we want. How do you wait, but not stand still? I've learned to pray and to study God's word and to trust that he is working things out in his own time. It's not easy to wait, and it doesn't necessarily ever get any easier. But when we take our focus off the object that has gained our attention and put it back on God, he will help us, strengthen us, and teach us through the waiting. He is still there, even as we wait.

Dear Lord, change my desires to be what you want for me. Thank you for being with me even as I wait for the things I want. I know you have my best in mind. Amen.

Day 19
Taking Off Our Old Selves

"Therefore, if anyone is in Christ, the new creation has come: The old has gone, the new is here!" (2 Co 5:17)

Have you ever watched a hermit crab change shells? My best friend, Casey, raises hermit crabs, and she has described the elaborate process to me. Hermit crabs will approach a new shell, spin it around, and examine it to make sure it doesn't have any holes in it. Then, they stick their heads and legs inside to examine the interior and see if it's smooth. If they like it, they will climb out of their old shell and into the new one. If it doesn't fit quite right, they will come out of it and put their old shell back on.

Casey discovered her love for hermit crabs a few years ago when she and her family brought back two hermit crabs from a vacation to the Gulf of Mexico. After arriving home, the crabs failed to thrive. She began doing research and found out that everything she'd been told by the store employees about caring for hermit crabs was wrong. She set out to find correct information and has since joined and moderated forums about properly caring for hermit crabs, made her own crab food, and created environments in which they can thrive. She even crochets hermit crab dolls and their removable shells to sell in her Etsy shop. She has rescued crabs from people who got them on vacation, but then couldn't take care of them.

The crabs' ritual when changing shells reminds me of the way we are "to put off your old self, which is being corrupted by its deceitful desires…and put on the new self, created to be like God in true righteousness and holiness" (Eph 4:22, 24). When we call on Jesus and ask him to save us, we are to leave our old lives behind, just as the crabs leave their old shells behind. There is a taking off of the old (things we should stop doing) and putting on of the new (things that we should start doing). Things we need to stop doing may include spending time with the wrong people, gossiping, or filling our minds with negative words or images. Things we need to start doing may include spending time reading God's word, praying, or looking for ways to help others. When we look to Jesus, he will give us the strength we need to move forward into our new life with him.

Dear Jesus, thank you for dying on the cross so that we can leave our old selves behind and find new life with you. Amen.

Day 20
Fiercely Protective

"But let all who take refuge in you be glad; let them ever sing for joy. Spread your protection over them, that those who love your name may rejoice in you." (Ps 5:11)

Lilly tugged at her leash as we approached a fellow walker. We walked in this park almost every morning, so the fast-moving woman coming toward us wasn't exactly a stranger. The closer she got, the more excited Lilly became. As the woman pulled up almost even with us, she smiled good morning and waved at Lilly.

Lilly, who until this time had calmly watched her approach, suddenly turned into Cujo. She stood on her hind legs and pawed the air like a miniature bear, growling and barking. Thankfully, the woman just laughed, complimented me on my cute dog, and kept walking. And this routine occurred every time we met for the rest of our walk.

Lilly is fiercely protective of me. When we walk, she will not allow anyone to come near us—including other dogs. She's a good defense mechanism against salespeople who come to my door. She barks so loudly that I can't hear their sales pitch, rattling the door with her little paws as she tries so hard to reach the person on the other side. I just apologize for the noise and tell them today's not their day. And they can't even get close enough to leave their promotional materials for fear that Lilly will bite them. I don't think she will, but why take that chance, right?

God is also fiercely protective of me. We can see in the Scriptures that God promised physical protection for the children of Israel in the Old Testament: "He will not let your foot slip—he who watches over you will not slumber" (Ps 121:3).

In the New Testament, God offers spiritual protection through the Holy Spirit: "But the Lord is faithful, and he will strengthen you and protect you from the evil one" (2 Thes 3:3). While he can still protect us from physical harm, the hard truth is that we all experience suffering of some kind, whether through the death of a family member or friend, chronic health problems, financial loss, or failed relationships. I don't believe God causes these trials, but he does use them to build our character and allow the fruit of the Spirit to manifest in us. He has promised us his peace to guard our hearts and minds (Phil 4:7).

Whatever you may be going through, remember that God is on your side: "If God is for us, who can be against us?" (Rom 8:31b) While he may not take the trials away, he will give us the strength we need to get through them. And he will carry us until we reach the other side.

Dear Jesus, thank you for being fiercely protective of me and for sending your Holy Spirit to help me endure times of trials. Give me strength to endure times of trials, and reveal your fruit in me. Amen.

Day 21
Greedy

"Then he said to them, 'Watch out! Be on your guard against all kinds of greed; life does not consist in an abundance of possessions.'" (Lk 12:15)

When I give Lilly a treat, she greedily snatches it out of my hand. I quickly move my fingers out of the way so that I don't get bitten. She's not trying to hurt me, but she's so eager to have the treat that she gets a little too enthusiastic. After she grabs the treat, she runs away and eats it as quickly as her little mouth will allow. While she's eating, she won't let me get close to her—she's afraid I'll try to steal it back. If I come too close to her, she picks up her treat and runs away. But as soon as she finishes eating, she comes back looking for more because one is never enough.

Often when God gives us a blessing, we act in much the same way. We grab the proffered blessing out of his hand, hoard it, and do not share with those around us. When someone comes close to us, we react with selfishness and impatience. We have no desire to be generous because we feel that God has bestowed this blessing on us and us alone.

However, God has commanded us to be cheerful givers: "Each of you should give what you have decided in your heart to give, not reluctantly or under compulsion, for God loves a cheerful giver" (2 Cor 9:7). We aren't born with an innate desire to help others. But we can pray and ask God to stir this desire within us.

We can help those around us and share with them, whether that means giving of our time, our money, or our talents. God has blessed each of us in different ways. I may be able to donate my time and energy to delivering meals at a local senior center, while someone who is homebound may be able pray for those receiving meals. Look for ways that God can use you, and then allow him to do so.

Dear Jesus, I pray that you'll give me a generous heart. Help me to want to love and help others and show me ways I can give from what you've given to me. Amen.

Day 22
The Goat Head Patch

"Then I will return to my place until they admit their guilt and turn to me. For as soon as trouble comes, they will earnestly search for me..." (Ho 5:15 NLT)

Lilly's favorite area in the yard contained a landmine of goat heads. These ferocious little stickers, no bigger than the end of my little finger, have needle-like projections. And, wow, do they hurt. They stick in the bottoms of shoes to get brought into the house and left on the floor to be stepped on later by bare feet—ouch!—and they sink deeply into my little dog's paws.

Whenever I noticed Lilly heading for the area that contained the goat heads, I would try to redirect her. Sometimes I caught her in time; other times, I didn't. When one sank into her paw, she would limp, looking at me so pitifully that I immediately knew what had happened. I would scoop her up and remove the offending sticker—often not without wounding myself in the process. As soon as I put her down, my usually brilliant dog would head right back to that area—so I would gently guide her to another part of the yard.

Often, we find ourselves refusing to give up a favorite sin in much the same way that Lilly refused to give up her favorite spot in the yard, even though she continued to get hurt. Our sin hurts us as well, and it hurts others and our relationship with Jesus. We may enjoy the sins of gossiping, lying, or lusting without even realizing how far we have gone and how many we have hurt. Because Jesus died to save us, we can confess these sins and turn them over for good. We don't have to keep running back to them. We can let go and let the Holy Spirit work in our lives, and we will be free.

Dear Jesus, please reveal to me my favorite sins and forgive me for hanging onto them. Thank you for your forgiveness and for not remembering my sins any longer. Help me to let go of these sins and not return to them again. Amen.

Day 23
Lessons Learned from a Cat

"God made the wild animals according to their kinds, the livestock according to their kinds, and all the creatures that move along the ground according to their kinds. And God saw that it was good..." (Gen 1:25)

My brother, Stoney, and his wife, Melissa, have a soft spot for animals. They are not just cat people or dog people, but they love all animals and have adopted cats and dogs of all sizes. I, on the other hand, am a dog person. I tolerate cats, but most of my affection is reserved for Lilly.

A while back, a friend asked for my help finding a home for his mom's cats (she had moved out of state). He had found homes for all but one very sweet, laid-back, coal-black cat, and he asked if my family would take care of him. My parents agreed since they feed cats that run free throughout the neighborhood. This cat joined the herd, finding a good cat friend in one of the more reticent black-and-white cats that never allowed us to get close to him. Eventually, this black cat helped his good friend out of his shell, and the black-and-white cat allowed us to get close enough to pet him—sometimes.

At first, it seemed silly to me to become so attached to these cats, but God can even use a cat to teach a truth about himself. In helping feed these cats, I realized that my attitude toward these animals was wrong. People are often like cats, which can be self-centered, demanding, and hard to love. It is easy to dismiss them and think that someone else will take care of them. However, God created them and loves them, and we should love them, too—people and cats! We are called to take care of the things God created—all things

(Gen 2:15). After he had made each part of creation, he "saw that it was good"—the last of these being humans (Gen 1:9, 12, 18, 21, 25, 31).

It took an unexpected opportunity taking care of a friend's cat to discover that I haven't been as open to loving others as I should be, and it's this chance that has allowed me to look beyond the gruff exterior some people present to show the love of Jesus to the hurting human inside.

Dear Jesus, help me look beyond a person's exterior to see the real person inside. Help me reach out and show your love. Amen.

Day 24
Is Stubbornness Ever a Virtue?

"Listen to me, you stubborn-hearted, you who are now far from my righteousness. I am bringing my righteousness near, it is not far away; and my salvation will not be delayed..." (Is 46:12-13)

We walked along the side of the road, Lilly trotting on the raised curb beside me. One of my many podcasts played in my ears as I took advantage of the nice weather and the opportunity to learn something new about the craft of writing. I wrapped Lilly's leash around my hand and wrist to ensure she couldn't suddenly break free and take off for parts unknown.

Suddenly, my hand holding the leash flew backwards, and I jolted to a stop. I looked around to find the cause, but I knew. It wasn't the first time—or even the thousandth time—that Lilly had decided to explore something in the opposite direction. I turned to face her, still holding the leash taut. She dug her little paws into the ground and strained her body away from me, giving me quite the side-eye. The amount of force in her little eleven-pound body surprised me. We stood this way for a moment, a standoff between me and my stubborn dog. But we both knew how it would end. I let out some slack in the leash, and she trotted happily to sniff a pile of dead leaves.

Lilly's stubbornness reminds me that I can be that way, too, especially if God asks me to step out of my comfort zone. I dig in my figurative heels and refuse to budge. Often, when God asks us to do something, we balk and try to run the other way. Or maybe we're walking along with him just fine until something catches our attention, and we take a detour to explore the new thing that we just had to have. We can be stubborn creatures when we want our own way, even if what we want isn't good for us. Sometimes even especially then.

Stubbornness can be a good thing when used correctly. In that case, it's called perseverance. When you know your calling, perseverance is a quality that will help you stick to your values and continue to pursue the calling God has for you.

God is gracious and patient. Even though God is in control, he has given us free will to make our own choices, sometimes to our own detriment. He waits for us to see that what he asks is for our good, even if we can't see it at the time. I'm so thankful for his patience and that he never leaves us, even in our stubbornness. He offers us a place of refuge when we turn back to him.

Dear Jesus, thank you for giving us free will to make our own choices and wisdom to make good ones. Even when we go our own way, you are still there, waiting patiently for us. Amen.

Day 25

The Benefits of Reading

"Rejoice with those who rejoice; mourn with those who mourn..." (Rom 12:15)

The cold months of winter were made for curling up with a cup of tea and a good book and of course, Lilly. When I read, Lilly likes to curl up in my lap (on top of a blanket, of course), or right next to my feet on the end of the recliner. She is always curious about what I'm reading – she gives the book a good sniff and then licks it a couple of times before giving her approval. When my mom reads the newspaper, Lilly jumps right in the middle of my mom's lap and steps on the paper before turning around as if she's reading, too.

I read for pleasure, but I also read to learn. Over the last year, I've read more nonfiction than ever before. I read a lot of Christian spiritual growth books and participate in Bible studies. I've grown enough in my walk with Christ to recognize when these books aren't theologically sound. Even so, I still receive a benefit from reading them because they cause me to dig into Scripture to discover for myself what the Bible really says.

We can learn a lot from reading, whether it's classic literature or escapist chick lit or a Bible study, or whether we read fiction or nonfiction. Books take us places we may never get to visit in person and allow us to meet people who are different than we are. Reading expands our perspective and our understanding of the world around us. One study has shown that reading literary fiction as opposed to genre fiction can increase our capacity for empathy.

When we read with an open mind, we can learn about the experiences that shape people, leading to empathy, compassion, and a greater understanding of others. As Christians, these are qualities we should all strive to embody in our own lives, and reading is a wonderful way to accomplish that.

Dear Jesus, please expand my capacity to understand others and feel empathy and compassion for whatever their situation may be. Amen.

Day 26
Training for the Marathon of Life

"All Scripture is God-breathed and is useful for teaching, rebuking, correcting and training in righteousness, so that the servant of God may be thoroughly equipped for every good work." (2 Ti 3:16-17)

When I got Lilly, people told me she couldn't be housebroken—that housebreaking a Yorkie isn't possible. I simply didn't believe that, so I conducted research to find the best methods for house training a Yorkie. I found a wealth of information online, and a common misconception about Yorkies seemed to be that the breed can't be trained. It's probably their innate stubbornness that perpetuates the myth. The consensus seemed to be that Yorkies could be trained, but with difficulty.

I sifted through the most reliable information and began training in a small area in the backyard. For a couple of weeks, I led Lilly to an area about five feet by five feet just outside the back door, and we didn't venture from that spot. Lilly would pull at the leash to explore the rest of the yard, but we stayed put until she had taken care of business. Every few weeks, I would expand her area until finally, after several months, she could explore the entire yard.

Sometimes, God works with us this way. He places a calling on our lives, but he asks us to train in increments, not allowing us to move onto the next step until we are completely comfortable in the area where he has placed us for the moment. It can be frustrating when we see the goal ahead, but we know we are still so far from reaching it. It takes persistence and dedication to follow God, and sometimes those attributes are in short supply. We become impatient with our progress, and we run into the open yard. If we rely on God's leading and timing, we know he will give us just what we need when we need it.

Dear Jesus, thank you for leading me to the area in life where you want me to be. Help me to wait on you and not run ahead just because I can see the end goal in sight. Show me how to wait for you to lead me there. Amen.

Day 27
The Wanderer

"Not long after that, the younger son got together all he had, set off for a distant country and there squandered his wealth in wild living...When he came to his senses, he said, 'How many of my father's hired servants have food to spare, and here I am starving to death!'" (Lk 15:13,17)

My childhood dog, Tanny, loved to roam. She followed me everywhere—around our yard, to my grandparents' house across town, to my cousins' place down the street. She even tried to follow me into the house on more than one occasion, but my mom promptly shooed her back outside.

Sometimes, Tanny would disappear for hours at a time, returning no worse for the wear at the end of the day. Like a child who saw the streetlights coming on, she knew when to go home. Since we lived in a small town of about 200 people, my parents didn't worry too much as long as she returned by nightfall. Occasionally, she stayed out beyond her curfew, prompting my dad to go searching for her. Each time, she returned bright and early on her own the next morning.

Her disappearing act reminds me of the prodigal son. Tanny would run off just as the prodigal son did. Both Tanny and the prodigal son returned home when they got hungry. And like the father who welcomed back the prodigal son, we did the same when Tanny returned.

In the same way, God welcomes us back when we wander off. He doesn't ask questions—he already knows where we've been and what we've done. He accepts us with open arms. That doesn't mean there won't be consequences for our actions. He doesn't remove the consequences, but he does forgive our sins, and he offers grace and mercy. He welcomes us back with a true homecoming.

Dear Jesus, please forgive me when I wander away. Thank you for allowing me to come back at any time, welcoming me and forgiving me no matter what I've done. Help me to follow you all the days of my life. Amen.

Day 28
Time to Play

"Before I formed you in the womb I knew you..." (Jer 1:5)

My brother, Stoney, and his wife, Melissa, live in Georgia with their furry family. The area where they live received snow for the first time in many years. My brother let his dogs out, and they had so much fun playing in the snow that they refused to go back inside. Zeke, the oldest dog at thirteen, played like a puppy, running and frolicking in the powdery snow.

When we're kids, we play without hesitation. We build, we draw, and we move, never giving a thought to what others might think. We play in the park or on the playground, making friends easily and not worrying about what we have in common or differences that may separate us. We revel in the fact that we all enjoy playing on the monkey bars or the swing set. It's enough to bind us together.

As we watch our animals play, we can remember that we once played with the same type of abandon. As we get older, we begin to conform, and we lose our ability to express our individuality freely. This sort of freedom is a gift from God, and Jesus paid the price for our freedom when he died on the cross: "So if the Son sets you free, you will be free indeed" (Jn 8:36).

The mundane cares of this world, the temptations and the unfulfilled desires, have a way of binding us in invisible chains that Jesus died to remove. As you go about your tasks today, ask the Lord to reveal to you those chains that bind you, and then ask him to break them so that you can embrace your freedom in Christ.

Dear Jesus, thank you for dying on the cross to set me free. Help me not to bind myself back in chains, but to live freely a life that honors you. Amen.

Day 29
Promise Keeper

Have I not commanded you? Be strong and courageous. Do not be afraid; do not be discouraged, for the Lord your God will be with you wherever you go. (Josh 1:9)

Lilly has been my furry, faithful companion for over eight years now. She trusts me completely—to feed her, to water her, to walk her, to play with her. I see it in her eyes when she rolls over for a belly rub and when she greets me as I walk in the door, dancing excitedly on her hind legs as she tries to lick my fingers. She never hesitates to bark for a treat or a trip outside because she knows that her wish will be granted. When we sit in my recliner, she burrows her head under my hand so that I will pet her and give her the attention she deserves.

Whether you have children or pets or both, you know what it is like to have someone depend on you. God wants us, his children, to depend on him the same way that Lilly depends on me. When I have a bad day, I can vent to him. I can express my frustration and my questions—he already knows anyway. When things go well, and even if they don't, I can praise him.

God is there when I call on him, and he provides for my every need. When I look back over my life, I see his hand guiding me and his protection over me. Even when I went my own way—maybe especially when I went my own way—he was still there, waiting for me to place him back in the top spot of my life. I see the fulfillment of promises to never leave me that he makes in his word (Dt 31:6, 8; Josh 1:6, 9; 1 Chr 28:20; Ps 37:28; Ps 94:14; Is 41:17; Is 42:16; Heb 13:5).

Like any flawed human, I have broken promises that I've made. Whether the break was intentional or not, broken promises lead to broken trust. We know that we can trust God not to break his promises to us because of his unchanging nature, his character, and his infinite wisdom, and because "God is not human, that he should lie, not a human being, that he should change his mind. Does he speak and then not act? Does he promise and not fulfill?" (Num 23:19)

What he promises, he will fulfill. And this is a promise we can count on.

Dear Jesus, thank you for fulfilling your promises to us. Help us to rely on you and trust you completely. Amen.

Day 30
Easing the Burden of Loneliness

"Turn to me and be gracious to me, for I am lonely and afflicted." (Ps 25:16)

Lilly came to me almost a year after my divorce. I had talked about adopting a pet, but I hadn't done anything about it yet. Instead, I had focused on work, volunteering, and earning my alternative teaching certificate. I had trouble adjusting to being alone after being married for so many years, and I threw myself into as many activities as I could find.

After I passed the last exam to earn my teaching certificate, I received a call from my brother, Stoney. At the time, he and Melissa, his wife, and my parents and I all lived in the same small town. He asked if I would stop by his house. He wanted to give me something to congratulate me. That "something" was Lilly.

The little six-month-old Yorkie won my heart as soon as I saw her. I hesitated to take her because I didn't have anything a puppy needed. Melissa gave me some food, a bed, and toys, so I had no excuse not to take her. I took her to visit my parents, and she was a hit with them as well. I took her home later that day, not really sure what to do with her at that point. We stared at each other for a while, and when I sat down in my recliner, she jumped up beside me, curled up on my lap, and took a nap. And so our relationship began.

As I took over caring for Lilly, I felt my loneliness decrease. Lilly both needed and demanded my attention. She helped me break the ice with co-workers who also had pets and with whom I hadn't had anything in common before.

When I started my blog seven months later, I wrote about Lilly and her antics. My stories about her were quite popular and led me to write a series of devotionals, including this one, years later.

After my divorce, I felt stressed by the number of changes that had occurred in my life so quickly. Taking care of Lilly decreased my stress level and changed my focus. No longer did I turn inward to my own problems. Lilly gave me a reason to get on the floor and play. I walked her every day, we went to visit my parents together, and I set up playdates with Stoney and Melissa's dogs. Lilly's companionship helped ease my loneliness. When I left the house, it didn't matter how long I was gone—five minutes or five hours— Lilly always greeted me at the door by standing on her hind legs and dancing in circles with excitement.

I had prayed for a companion, and God sent Lilly. I have no doubt that he used Lilly to help me heal. As I continue to weather life's ups and downs, I'm thankful for her constant presence and the reminder that God cares for us in our pain and loneliness. He will always provide a way through it.

Dear Jesus, thank you for the rambunctious ball of fur that you sent to me in Lilly. Thank you for her constant companionship and love. Help me to remember your faithfulness. Amen.

Acknowledgements

Without the support of my family and friends, this book would not have been possible. Thank you to everyone who believed in me enough to buy the books in the Echoes of Joy series and who have encouraged me to keep writing. To each person who has asked about the progress on this book and told me she can't wait to read it—thank you!

A special thank you goes to my parents and brother, Stoney, and his wife, Melissa, for their love of animals and allowing me to tell their stories in this book. I also want to thank my mom, Lola Hart, and my friends, Michelle Buckner, Amy Fergueson, Taffy Henderson, Rebekah Rhoades, and Casey Witvoet, for reading through this book and providing feedback. And thank you to my friend and editor, Michael Matthews, for encouraging me to continue writing and for being such a great editor.

About the Author

Staci Mauney is a freelance writer and editor and indie author. She is the co-owner of Prestige Prose, a freelance writing and editing company. As an author, she has written three devotionals in the Echoes of Joy series: *Echoes of Joy: 30 Days of Experiencing God's Grace, Echoes of Joy: A Daily Devotional for Christmas*, and *Echoes of Joy: Growing Closer to God*, all of which can be found on her website at stacimauney.com. Her Yorkshire terrier, Lilly, is the main character in her devotionals and her blog, which can also be found on her website. She has had short stories published in *Chicken Soup for the Shopper's Soul; Owl Hootings, Vol. II; Oklahoma: The Fountain of the Heartland*; and the *OWFI Report* and has worked as a content writer for *Oklahoma Farm and Ranch* magazine. Staci volunteers for a variety of organizations in her local community. She has been a member of the Oklahoma Writers' Federation, Inc. (OWFI) since 2007 and is serving as the 2019 OWFI president.

Made in the USA
Lexington, KY
15 September 2018